INTERNATIONAL TAX PLANNING

Tax Guide on Offshore Companies and Tax Havens

JEAN FRANCO
FERNÁNDEZ CLARK

OFFSHORE AFFAIRS

The information contained in this book comes from personal experience only and the author's personal point of view, and it, in any way, shall not constitute nor be a substitute for legal, tax, or financial advice. The content herein is for entertainment purposes only, and its content might be incorrect or incomplete. You must get advice from a licensed attorney, accountant, or financial services provider.

Copyright © 2024 by Jean Franco Fernández Clark

All rights reserved. No part of this publication may be reproduced, distributed, or transmitted in any form or by any means, including photocopying, recording, or other electronic or mechanical methods, without the prior written permission of the publisher, except in the case of brief quotations embodied in critical reviews and certain other noncommercial uses permitted by copyright law. For permission requests, write to the author.

ISBN:

9798334073852

International Tax Planning: Tax Guide for Offshore Companies and Tax Havens

Table of Contents

INTERNATIONAL TAX PLANNING: TAX GUIDE FOR OFFSHORE COMPANIES AND TAX HAVENS 3

INTRODUCTION 9
    WHAT IS INTERNATIONAL TAX PLANNING? 12
    WHAT IS TAX AVOIDANCE VS TAX EVASION? 12

CHAPTER 1 TAX RESIDENCY 14
    DIFFERENCE BETWEEN BEING A TAX OR NON-TAX RESIDENT 15
        Tax Residency implications 15
        Non-Residents 15
    COMPANY AND INDIVIDUAL TAX RESIDENCY 16
        Company Tax Residency 16
        Residency by Company Permanent Establishment 17
        Residency by Place of Incorporation 18
        Tax residency if a company meets one of the following 18
    SOME TAX HAVENS DETERMINE THEIR TAX RESIDENCY BY PLACE OF MANAGEMENT AND CONTROL, AND NOT OF INCORPORATION. 19
    COMPANY TAX RESIDENCY BY PLACE OF MANAGEMENT AND CONTROL 20
        How to avoid being a tax resident based on the jurisdiction of control and management 21
    INDIVIDUAL TAX RESIDENCY 21
        Tax Residency by Physical Presence 22
        Center of Vital Interests: 22
        Tax residency by Citizenship 22
    HOW TO STOP BEING AN INDIVIDUAL TAX RESIDENT. 23
    DUAL OR MULTIPLE TAX RESIDENCY FOR COMPANIES AND INDIVIDUALS.

....23

INDIVIDUAL MULTIPLE TAX RESIDENCY. 24
COMPANY MULTIPLE TAX RESIDENCY 24
NOT BEING A TAX RESIDENCY OF ANY JURISDICTION 25
BEING A TAX RESIDENT BUT NOT PAYING TAXES 25
THE IMPORTANCE OF THE DETERMINATION OF TAX RESIDENCY 26
HOW DO CORPORATE SERVICE PROVIDERS, LAWYERS, AND BANKS DETERMINE THE INDIVIDUAL'S TAX RESIDENCY? 26
HOW REDUCE YOUR TAX BILL OR AVOID TAXES RELATED TO TAX RESIDENCY: 26

Having the company be owned by a nominee shareholder who resides in a tax haven. 27
Declaration of Trust deed 27
Providing the most beneficial proof of address 28
Holding more than one passport 29

CHAPTER 2 OFFSHORE COMPANIES AND TAX HAVENS 30

WORLDWIDE VS TERRITORIAL TAX SYSTEM 30
WORLDWIDE TAX SYSTEM 31
TERRITORIAL TAX SYSTEM: 31
MIXED OR HYBRID TAX SYSTEM: 32
TAX HAVENS AND OFFSHORE COMPANIES 32
WHAT IS AN OFFSHORE COMPANY? 32
TAX HAVENS 33
  What is a tax haven? 33
  PURE TAX HAVENS 33

CHAPTER 3 TAXES 35

SOURCE PRINCIPLE IN INTERNATIONAL TAXATION 36

INCOME TAX: 37

BUSINESS INCOME TAX - TYPE OF ENTITY 37
    Corporations 38
    LLCs, Partnerships 38
    Some ways to reduce your income tax 38
    Increase your costs and expenses 39
    Earning this income through an offshore company. 40
    Black and Gray Labeled Tax Havens Lists 41

CAPITAL GAINS TAX 41

REALIZED CAPITAL GAINS TAX 41
CAPITAL GAINS TAX EXEMPTION 42
NOT SELLING YOUR ASSETS IN ORDER TO AVOID INCURRING INTO A
REALIZED CAPITAL GAINS EVENT 42
FACTORS DETERMINING IF AN INCOME IS CAPITAL GAIN OR REGULAR
BUSINESS INCOME 43
    *Percentage of overall income to determine if sale of asset is capital gain or regular
    income* 43
    *How long you hold an asset might determine if the income would be treated as capital
    gains or regular income* 43
TRUST TO AVOID CAPITAL GAINS TAX OR INHERITANCE TAX 44
HOW AND WHY DO RICH PEOPLE OR MILLIONAIRES DO NOT PAY TAXES?
BUY BORROW DIE TAX STRATEGY 44
    The Contrast - Getting Paid in Salary 45
    How can anyone benefit from this? 46
    Important considerations: 46

WITHHOLDING TAX 46

WAYS TO AVOID WITHHOLDING TAX 48
    Tax treaties. 48
    Forming a tax resident company in a Country A 48
    A specific option to avoid withholding taxes from the European Union 48

EXIT TAX 49

TAX TREATY 50

TREATY SHOPPING 51

    WHAT IS TREATY SHOPPING? 51

    TAX TREATY RESIDENT STATUS 52

        Minimum tax rate required 53

        Maintenance price of low tax companies 54

        Not all Low Tax Jurisdictions are subject to economic substance requirements to benefit from their tax residency and tax treaties. 55

ECONOMIC SUBSTANCE REQUIREMENTS 55

PROFIT SHIFTING 57

    BASE EROSION: 57

    PROFIT SHIFTING STRATEGIES 58

        Intellectual Property 58

        Services 59

        Loans 60

CFC RULES 61

TRANSFER PRICING 62

    WHAT ARE RELATED ENTITIES UNDER THE TRANSFER PRICING RULES? ...63

    ARM'S LENGTH PRINCIPLE 64

    TAX INFORMATION EXCHANGE AGREEMENTS 65

    NOW THAT YOU KNOW THE BASICS OF INTERNATIONAL TAX PLANNING, LET'S REVIEW ONE OF MOST POPULAR INTERNATIONAL TAX STRATEGIES 66

    DOUBLE IRISH DUTCH SANDWICH TAX AVOIDANCE EXPLAINED 66

FINAL THOUGHTS 69

COMPANY IMPORTANT LINKS 70

    OFFSHORE AFFAIRS WEBSITE 70

    TWITTER 70

    YOUTUBE 70

    OFFSHORE AFFAIRS LINKEDIN 71

    JEAN FRANCO FERNANDEZ CLARK'S CONTACT 71

    LINKEDIN 71

    X/ TWITTER 71

Introduction

By just opening an offshore company in a tax haven you are not guaranteed not paying taxes in any jurisdiction. This might have been a reality in the past when it was just as easy as opening an offshore company, and you knew you were guaranteed that you would not pay taxes.

Nowadays tax havens have been forced by third-party jurisdictions and multilateral organizations to implement rules, instruments, and regulations to avoid or facilitate tax evasion, and money laundering.

Despite the above, it is still 0% possible to avoid paying taxes at all, nonetheless, it is now a more complex procedure, which is why it is essential that you are aware of these rules, regulations, and legal instruments to be able to reduce your tax base and obtain tax freedom and tax optimization.

The purpose of this book is to provide insight into the local and international tax concepts involved and related to international companies, offshore companies, international tax planning, tax havens, and more.

There are several factors to take into consideration when assessing your local and international tax affairs, as not only your tax status plays a role, but also the tax status of the payor, if the jurisdiction is a black or gray-listed jurisdiction, instruments **implemented by jurisdictions to avoid the artificial transfer of income or artificial tax base erosion, CFC Rules, Transfer Pricing Rules, and more.**

For example, if you live in a jurisdiction where you don't pay income tax as an individual, let's say Dubai, U.A.E, and open a company in the British Virgin Islands, and this company receives royalty payments from the U.S.A., the U.S.A. will tax your royalty profits at a 30% tax rate.

In the opposite scenario, if you live in a high-tax country, let's say the U.K. Canada, Japan, U.S.A, etc., and you open an Offshore Company in a tax haven, and this is a shell company with no office space or employees (substance) in the jurisdiction of formation, this would not be enough to legally not pay taxes or defer the payment of taxes in your country of individual tax residency as most likely the Controlled Foreign Company Rules (CFC Rules) would apply to you, and your country of tax residency will tax the income of the BVI company as if the net income of your offshore company was distributed and paid to you, even if you did not take the earnings out of the company.

There are multiple ways to avoid paying these taxes, but first, you or your advisor must play by the rules and regulations to be able to find the loopholes or legally circumvent the regulations to legally avoid and not pay taxes.

In this book we will provide insight, so you understand these regulations and some ways to avoid paying taxes, as naturally, someone who is not an international tax lawyer generally is not well aware of all these instruments used by jurisdictions for individuals and companies to avoid paying taxes, especially if it is their first time opening an offshore company.

Each type of tax has its own nature and ways to optimize/avoid it. That is when international tax planning comes into play, where we take into consideration all the possible aspects that might affect your tax situation, as just opening an offshore company in a random 0% tax jurisdiction will not suffice.

Each concept will vary depending on jurisdiction to jurisdiction, and in some jurisdictions, some concepts might not even exist or not be implemented.

This book focuses on providing you with ways to avoid, legally, these regulations and taxes. Herein we will mostly cover the following topics, which will include ways to legally circumvent or avoid them:

- Tax residency for companies and individuals.
- Worldwide and territorial tax systems.
- Offshore Companies and Tax Havens.
- Income and capital gains tax, and ways to reduce it or

avoid it.

- Withholding tax
- Tax Information Exchange Agreements
- Exit tax.
- Controlled Foreign Companies (CFC Rules).
- Economic Substance Requirements (ESR)
- Transfer Pricing.
- Tax treaties and treaty shopping.

What is international tax planning?

International tax planning is legally optimizing your individual and company tax bill by being aware of all the concepts involved in international taxation, like Tax Residency, CFC Rules, Tax System, Economic Substance Requirements, use of tax havens, and understanding the local tax aspects and rules, as by truly understanding the rules we can find a way to avoid paying taxes legally.

What is tax avoidance vs tax evasion?

Tax avoidance is optimizing your tax bill by playing by the rules, hence profiting from the loopholes in the jurisdictions' tax codes and international instruments subscribed, taking advantage of their provisions.

On the other hand, Tax Evasion is illegally not paying taxes by engaging in illegal behavior like submitting false reports, hiding and not reporting bank accounts, and company ownership where you are supposed to report the existence of such money or company.

Chapter 1

Tax Residency

The concept of tax residency is highly important, as this is the basis of whether a type of tax and set of rules and regulations will be applied to you or your company.

Being a Tax Resident or Non-Tax Resident will determine if a country has a right to tax you, if certain taxes will be applied to you, or if withholding tax is to be applied to income sourced from that jurisdiction as a non-resident.

Being a tax resident of a certain country means you will be treated as such pursuant to that jurisdiction's tax code. Being a tax resident does not mean you are a resident for immigration purposes as you can be tax resident but not legally a resident of that jurisdiction.

An individual or company being a tax resident or a non-tax resident in a jurisdiction does not mean that you will be taxed or not taxed in that jurisdiction for that income. Depending on each income type, an income will be subject to taxes or not to tax residents or non-tax residents.

Difference between being a tax or non-tax resident

Tax Residency implications

Being taxed as a tax resident, in case your income is subject to taxes as a resident, will in theory allow you to deduct costs and expenses, this is the only benefit from being a tax either.

Being a tax resident in a jurisdiction might sometimes mean you will pay taxes in that jurisdiction on your worldwide income (we will discuss this further in the worldwide vs territorial tax system subchapter)

In the offshore world, sometimes forming a company or being a tax resident in a jurisdiction that has very low-income tax will allow you to reduce your overall tax bill. (we will discuss further in the tax treaties and treaty shopping subchapter).

Non-Residents

Being a non-tax resident in a jurisdiction does not mean you will not be taxed if you receive income sourced from that jurisdiction. It all would depend on the payment concept and on the jurisdiction tax code, as always.

In general, when you are a non-tax resident, if you receive income for providing professional services while physically outside of that jurisdiction, the payor would not withhold income tax, but if payment concept is Royalty or Interests (from loans or bank deposits) it might be subject to taxes, and the problem with this is that your taxable base will be your gross income, without allowing you do deduct expenses on that income.

When an income is subject to tax to a non-tax resident because such income is sourced from that jurisdiction, the latter will levy a withholding tax. (We will discuss the withholding tax below).

If the income is subject to withholding tax, you can reduce this by either creating a tax resident company there and doing tax planning which will allow you to deduct costs and expenses, or by claiming tax treaty benefits by creating a company in a jurisdiction that has a double taxation avoidance treaty with this second jurisdiction.

Company and individual tax residency

Company Tax Residency

In general, for companies, tax residency is determined by the Country of incorporation, and/or country of management (where annual meetings are held and where decisions are taken).

Sometimes, depending on the jurisdictions' tax code, your

company could be a tax resident in two or more jurisdictions at the same time, that is the case if country A considers tax resident a company by country of incorporation, and country B considers a company tax resident by way of place of management.

Residency by Company Permanent Establishment

Your company can also be a tax resident in another jurisdiction if you have a permanent establishment (PE) there, or it has representatives who sign contracts on the company behalf there.

For example, if you have a company formed in the Cayman Islands, and this company opens a restaurant, factory, shop, warehouse, etc., in London (for example), the London Tax Authority (HMRC) will treat the portion of income earned through this permanent establishment as sourced from the U.K. (logically), and will only tax the portion of this income earned through this Permanent Establishment, but not the overall Cayman Islands company income.

Another way you can have a Permanent Establishment is by having a dependent agent with authority to conclude contracts, such as an employee or representative, who has the authority to conclude contracts on behalf of the company can create a PE. The agent must regularly exercise this authority in the jurisdiction.

Companies may seek to avoid creating a PE to minimize their tax liability. Strategies for this include fragmenting activities into smaller, preparatory, or auxiliary functions that do not constitute a PE. Another common strategy is engaging agents who operate independently and do not have the authority to conclude contracts on behalf of the company. The exact details, and the ways to circumvent being a tax resident, will be found in that jurisdiction's tax code.

Residency by Place of Incorporation

Some jurisdictions deem a company as a tax resident if incorporated or formed there as one of the factors to determine tax residency.

Tax residency if a company meets one of the following

There are jurisdictions that have a mix of features that determine if a company is a tax resident there. For example, some jurisdictions state that a company will be a tax in a certain jurisdiction there if the company:

- Is formed in that jurisdiction.

- Has its Management and Control in that jurisdiction (even though the company is not formed there).

- Has a Permanent Establishment there.

Not all jurisdictions of course have that full provision. Some may implement it partially, or fully, depending on the specific tax code.

For example, in Singapore companies formed in Singapore are not considered tax residents, but companies managed and having its place of management in Singapore are considered tax residents, so before the eyes of Singapore's tax code, a company formed in the BVI that has place of control and management in Singapore, will be considered a tax resident in Singapore, but a company formed in Singapore but having its place of Management and Control in the BVI will not be considered a tax resident.

Some tax havens determine their tax residency by place of management and control, and not of incorporation.

It is a common practice in a lot of tax havens to not consider companies formed in their jurisdictions as tax resident, they consider tax residency of a company based on where the company is managed and exercised its control, meaning if the company is controlled and managed from its jurisdiction, they will deem that company as a tax resident.

This concept is beneficial as it allows you to have an offshore company with no tax residency on its place of formation (i.e. Cayman Islands, BVI, Belize, etc.) This way, for example, you could form a company in the British Virgin Islands, and report this company as not having its place of Management and Control in the BVI, making this company a non-tax resident in the BVI, and hence not being subject to the Economic Substance Requirements (we will discuss about the Economic Substance Requirements below)

Company Tax Residency by Place of Management and Control

Tax residency based on the place of management and control is a principle that determines where a company is considered a resident for tax purposes by focusing on the location of its key decision-making activities. This typically involves the location where the board of directors meets and makes strategic decisions, where the company's executive directors and senior management operate, and where major corporate policies and directions are set. Jurisdictions like the United Kingdom and Australia apply this concept by considering a company tax resident if its central management and control occurs within their borders. Similarly, India uses the place of effective management (POEM) to ascertain residency for companies whose significant management decisions are made within the country. The implications of this principle are profound, affecting a company's tax liability and potentially leading to dual residency issues where a company is considered resident in multiple countries, thus subjecting it to double taxation. To mitigate such risks, Double Taxation Avoidance Agreements (DTAAs) often include tiebreaker rules favoring the country of effective management. Adherence to these rules is crucial for companies with cross-border operations to ensure compliance and optimize their tax position.

How to avoid being a tax resident based on the jurisdiction of control and management

Avoiding tax residency based on the center of management and control involves strategic planning and executing management activities across multiple locations. One effective approach is to decentralize decision-making by distributing key strategic decisions across various countries. This can be achieved by holding board meetings and executive sessions in different jurisdictions and ensuring that senior executives and decision-makers spend significant time working outside the target jurisdiction. Establishing the company's main operational headquarters and key administrative functions in another jurisdiction can further support the claim that the center of management and control is not concentrated in the undesired location.

Individual Tax Residency

From the individual point of view, you can be a tax resident in a country by virtue of your nationality (in general, for those citizens in countries with a worldwide tax system), or by virtue of the time you have spent in certain territory.

Tax Residency by Physical Presence

In general, you are a tax resident in a jurisdiction if you spend 180 days in a calendar year therein.

Center of Vital Interests:

Some jurisdictions even consider you a tax resident there if your personal center of vital interest is there, which includes where your personal and economic ties are strongest. This could involve the location of family, employment, business activities, and social connections.

Tax residency by Citizenship

Some jurisdictions determine your tax residency based on your citizenship. For example, if you are a U.S. Person, you will always be a tax resident in the U.S. even if you have never lived there, or have been out of the U.S. for decades.

Only thing is that if you live outside of the U.S. they give you a Foreign Earned Income tax exclusion, meaning if you reside outside of the U.S. and your income does not exceed certain threshold, which is below US$120,000 per year for year 2023, you will not be taxed in the U.S., but if your income exceeds that threshold you will be taxed, even if you don't have any type of link to the U.S. besides your nationality.

How to stop being an individual tax resident.

To stop being a tax resident in a jurisdiction it will depend on that jurisdiction's tax code and what factor specifically makes you a tax resident there.

If you are a tax resident in a jurisdiction because of your nationality, you will have to give up your nationality/passport, and acquire a second citizenship; if you are a tax resident because you have your center of vital interest there, you will have to close all your companies, bank accounts, sell your house, etc., to avoid this; if you are a tax resident because of the physical presence test, you would just have to not be physically in that jurisdiction for a period of time above the threshold.

In most cases, especially those with a worldwide tax system, you will have to perform an exit tax procedure, where to cease being a tax resident you need to pay any Capital Gains tax accrued.

Dual or multiple tax residency for companies and individuals.

As we mentioned before, each jurisdiction has its own definition of a tax resident, and there are cases where you are a tax resident even if you don't live there.

That is one of the reasons why Double Taxation Avoidance Agreements exist, nonetheless, not all jurisdictions have Double Taxation Avoidance Agreements (DTAA) with all jurisdictions, and some jurisdictions do not even have a DTAA with any other jurisdiction.

Individual multiple tax residency.

It will depend on your jurisdictions' specific tax codes, but for example, if you are a U.S. Citizen or Green Card holder ("U.S. Person" for tax purposes), or a Canadian or U.K. tax resident who has not performed an exit tax procedure, you will also be a tax resident in the jurisdiction where you physically reside.

Company Multiple Tax Residency

A company can be a tax resident in, for example, the following scenario:

It is formed in a jurisdiction where tax residency is based on the country of incorporation/formation, and

It also has its Place of Management and Control in another jurisdiction, where one of the factors that determine a company's tax residency based on place of Management and Control.

A way to avoid this, is to of course understand the tax residency rules of each jurisdiction involved in your tax and offshore affairs to avoid being a tax resident in one, two, or more jurisdictions.

In cases where there is a multiple tax residency status, a tax treaty between two jurisdictions will allow you to only be taxed in a jurisdiction. These jurisdictions will surely not have the same tax rate, which is why sometimes it is better to create the tax residency status in the jurisdiction that gives you a much lower tax rate.

Not being a tax residency of any jurisdiction

Just as you can be a tax resident in multiple jurisdictions, it can also happen that you are not a tax resident of any jurisdiction.

This is 100% legal and can be accomplished by avoiding the specific factors that might make you a tax resident in one or more jurisdictions.

Being a tax resident but not paying taxes

Additionally, you can also be a tax resident in a jurisdiction, and not pay taxes. This is accomplished by your company or you personally being a tax resident in a tax haven.

The importance of the determination of tax residency

Tax residency is truly highly important, as tax residency will be the cornerstone to determine if you will be subject to all these rules and taxation. For example, the U.K. will not tax you on your worldwide income if you are not a tax resident there, hence the U.K.'s C.F.C Rules, transfer pricing rules, etc., will not be applied to you at the individual level.

How do corporate service providers, lawyers, and banks determine the individual's tax residency?

For your offshore affairs, proof of address can be determined by the document you provide as proof of address in the form of utility bill or bank statement,

If you are a U.S. Person, it is a little bit more complicated, as even if you provide a proof of address in a tax haven, you would still be considered a U.S. tax resident.

How reduce your tax bill or avoid taxes related to tax residency:

There are ways to avoid paying taxes by ignoring these rules by providing the most convenient proof of address or appointing a nominee shareholder, owner, and manager(s), these might or might not be considered illegal depending on your specific jurisdiction, nonetheless, we will mention some ways some people use to avoid all these rules and regulations.

Disclaimer: we are not endorsing or promoting illegal strategies to avoid taxes, we are just providing this information for educational and information purposes only.

Having the company be owned by a nominee shareholder who resides in a tax haven.

To avoid all these regulations in their home country, some people hire nominee shareholders located in tax havens, this way deceiving tax authorities.

Declaration of Trust deed

A nominee shareholder is a person that appears on the public records as the holder of the company's shares. This is to keep the identity of the company beneficiary out of the public eye, hence, for a fee, a person appears on the public records as the owner, but this nominee is not granted neither administrative nor management powers.

For these types of situations, the beneficiary and the nominee sign a "Declaration of Trust" where the Nominee states he or she is holding the shares as a trustee of the beneficiary and agrees to transfer all the shares to the beneficiary, or to assign the shares to another person as requested by the beneficiary, upon and pursuant to the beneficiary's request. This Declaration of Trust is an internal document, not disclosed to or with third parties.

The Nominee Shareholder also states that she/he holds the dividends and interest accrued on trust for the beneficiary, which shall be transferred to the Beneficiary as requested by him/her.

If the Nominee Shareholder transfers the shares without the Beneficiary consent, or refuses to transfer the shares as per the Shareholder's instruction, the nominee can get sued, pay an indemnification to the beneficiary, and such transaction will be void!

There are laws that requires the disclosure of the final beneficiary of the shares and the funds, so from a legal point of view this nominee director is just to keep the beneficiary owner's name out of the public eye.

Providing the most beneficial proof of address

There are several legal ways that an individual can have a proof of address in several jurisdictions, for example, you could have a proof of address in France, but also a proof of address from the U.A.E. When going under an AML/KYC procedure, an individual could provide the proof of address as a way of utility bill or bank statement that is the most beneficial for his tax and privacy situation.

Holding more than one passport

If you have 2 or more passports, some people provide the passport that best fits their tax situation.

Chapter 2

Offshore Companies and Tax Havens

Worldwide VS Territorial Tax System

A big factor to that will determine your overall taxation, hence your international tax strategy, is if your jurisdiction of tax residency taxes you individually or your company on its worldwide or territorial system. These differences are known as tax system, where a country has a Worldwide Tax System, and the other has a Territorial Tax System.

Generally, one of the features that make a tax haven a "tax haven" is that they have a territorial tax system, meaning that they only tax companies formed there on their income generated from sourced within their jurisdiction. There are other factors that make a tax haven a tax haven, besides having a territorial tax system, but we will discuss that below in the tax havens subchapter.

Worldwide Tax System

A country with a worldwide tax system will tax its tax resident individuals and tax resident companies on the income generated therein, and the income generated in another territory. For example, You (personally or your Company) are a tax resident in Country A. Since country A has a Worldwide Tax System, you will pay taxes (or Country A will try to tax you) on profits generated in Country A, and in Countries from B to Z, even if the income was generated through a company formed in another country with no relation to or presence in Country A, except in those jurisdictions that Country A has a Tax Treaty with.

In these types of countries, it is a little bit more difficult to avoid taxes as, for example, if you are a U.S. citizen, you have lived in Thailand for several years, and are employed in and work from Thailand, you will be required to still pay income on your wages received in Thailand (after a certain threshold is met). I am not trying to say that there are not tax planning strategies to reduce your tax base, but you get the idea.

Territorial Tax System:

Generally, jurisdictions with a Territorial Tax System only levy tax on those profits generated in that jurisdiction. Each jurisdiction has its rule to determine if a profit has been generated therein. Just as an example, and in general, if the services or products are not provided within the territory of incorporation, the services income will not be taxed, even if the services are provided through a company incorporated there.

In the case of citizens, they will not pay tax on income generated abroad or from foreign sources.

Mixed or Hybrid Tax System:

Some countries have a mixed tax system, where for example natural persons are not taxed on their worldwide income but companies are, which is the case of Nicaragua, for example.

Tax Havens and Offshore Companies

What is an offshore company?

An Offshore company is just a company considered a non-tax resident according to that jurisdiction's tax code, regardless if this company is formed in a high tax country like France, Canada, Australia, etc.

The concept of an offshore company is not a company formed in a tax haven, even though the term has been colloquially used to refer to companies formed in low tax, secret, and uncooperative jurisdictions

So, we can conclude that an Offshore Company is a company formed or incorporated in a foreign jurisdiction.

Tax Havens

What is a tax haven?

Technically, a tax haven is a jurisdiction where a tax is significantly lower than the tax rate charged by another jurisdiction. So for example, if "Jurisdiction A" levies a 20% income tax rate, and "Jurisdiction B" levies a 9% income tax rate, before the eyes of "Jurisdiction A", "Jurisdiction B" is a tax haven.

A country does not need to levy a 0% income tax to be considered a tax haven.

We used the income tax rate as an example, but if for example a jurisdiction has a 30% income tax rate but has 0% capital gains tax, this can also be considered a tax haven.

For example, Liechtenstein has a high-income tax rate, but might not charge a royalty tax on royalty payments made or received, so Liechtenstein can be considered as a tax haven for Royalty Taxes.

Pure Tax Havens

When a jurisdiction levies a 0% tax rate on most, if not all, types of earnings, like income tax, capital gains, inheritance tax, property tax, sales tax., etc., they are usually denominated as "pure tax havens".

Chapter 3
Taxes

There are several types of taxes depending on your income type, and their source, tax rate, type of source, and ways to reduce it will depend on the specific tax codes involved, as, especially when dealing with international transactions, two or more jurisdictions tax codes are involved.

It is important to note that we are analyzing scenarios where the person or company is subject to taxes. Of course, if the individual resides in a tax haven or the company is formed in a tax haven, the person or company will not be subject to taxes, but there are other tax implications, as for example, the individual and company might be tax residents in a tax haven, but if they have income sourced from other jurisdictions that is subject to taxes there, then they will be subject to taxes in that jurisdiction, hence a more complex strategy is required to reduce the same base or tax rate.

Some countries have implemented several instruments to avoid the artificial deferral of income to no tax or low tax jurisdictions, like Controlled Foreign Companies rules, Common Reporting

Standards, transfer pricing rules, Economic Substance Requirements, tax information sharing agreements, etc.

Source Principle in International Taxation.

The term "source" in international taxation refers to the origin or the place where the specific type of income is generated. It is a legal concept used by countries to assert their right to tax an income. This right is based on the principle that income should be taxed where it is earned, where the economic activities that produced the income take place, or where the assets that generate the income are located.

Types of Income and Their Source

Employment or professional services Income: The source of employment or professional services income is typically the place where the employment is performed. For example, if an individual residing in country A works or provides services to a company or individual residing in country B, the income will not be sourced in Country B as the person is provide the services outside of Country B, even if the payor is a person tax resident in Country B.

Business Income: The source of business income is usually the location where the business activities are conducted. This can be determined by factors such as the place of management and the place where contracts are executed, and mostly where the business income is physically performed from.

Investment Income: The source of investment income, such as dividends, interest, and capital gains, is often tied to the location of the payer or the location of the investment itself. For example, interest income paid by a bank in Country A to a resident of Country B is typically sourced in Country A.

Royalties: The source of royalty income is generally the place where the intellectual property is used. If a company in Country A licenses its technology to a company in Country B, and the technology is used in Country B, the royalty income is sourced in Country B.

Income tax:

This income tax will tax your income from business activities or trade. This is the income generated from your active business line, and taxes your net income, not your gross income.

Income tax treatment will be differentiated on income tax earned by an individual or by a company.

Business Income Tax - Type of entity

It is worth mentioning that depending on the type of business entity, the company will be subject or not subject to income tax.

Corporations

In general, corporations or companies held by shares, are subject to Corporate Tax, and when this corporation pays dividends to the shareholders, the shareholder will pay taxes on this dividend on its personal income tax return, or might be subject to withholding tax in case the shareholder is a non-resident in the jurisdictions where the corporation is incorporated, and given that the corporation levies taxes on dividends paid to non-residents.

LLCs, Partnerships

These entities are what is called a pass-through or tax transparent entities, meaning that the LLCs do not submit an income tax return, but the income is passed to the owner(s) and the owner(s) would pay taxes in the jurisdiction of formation only if the income earned by the company is sourced from the formation jurisdiction, or if the owner is a tax resident in that jurisdiction.

The payment made from the LLC or Partnership is called Distribution, not Dividends, hence this payment will not be classified as Dividend, what will also help you avoid the withholding tax on Dividends.

Some ways to reduce your income tax

As explained above, there are several things to take into consideration in order to reduce your income tax, and each scenario will be different, like the jurisdiction where the company is formed and its tax code, type of entity, your tax residency, and if the jurisdiction where the corporation is formed has a double taxation avoidance Agreement with the jurisdiction you are a tax resident in (in case your company is formed in a jurisdiction different from where you reside).

If you are subject to income tax as an individual or company, either because you or your company is a tax resident in a jurisdiction that levies income tax on its residents, or because the source of payments levies withholding tax on the specific type of income you are receiving, the following are some basic ways you can explore to reduce your tax base.

Increase your costs and expenses

By increasing your costs and expenses, your net income will be reduced, and your income will be subject to a lower rate in case the jurisdiction taxes corporate income tax at a progressive tax rate (meaning the higher the income, higher the tax rate), and also your tax rate will be applied to a lower amount of income.

In this case, you must be aware of the following concepts:
- Withholding tax: in the event the money is sent abroad to an offshore company.
- Transfer Pricing Rules: in case the offshore company where the money is sent to is owned, directly or indirectly

by the same Royalty Payor.

Earning this income through an offshore company.

One option is to earn your income through an offshore company, this way the company will be located in a more tax-friendly jurisdiction, where most, if not all, income will be exempt from income tax.

This allows you to manage your company business and tax affairs in a more tax-friendly jurisdiction, with fewer regulations, and less costs and expenses control or scrutiny compared as if this company was in your country of tax residency.

What to be aware of: withholding tax, as if this offshore company has income that is deemed to be sourced from a certain jurisdiction, it will be taxed at the general withholding tax rate, unless there is a tax treaty with the jurisdiction where the offshore company is formed, and the jurisdiction where the income generated is sourced.

If the income is subject to withholding tax in its source jurisdiction, to reduce this withholding tax it is necessary to form an offshore company in a jurisdiction that has a tax treaty with this tax withholding jurisdiction.

Black and Gray Labeled Tax Havens Lists

There is something colloquially referred to as the tax havens black and gray list. This list refers to those jurisdictions listed by specific jurisdictions or multilateral organizations as uncooperative for tax evasion and anti-money laundering purposes.

The effects of forming a company in a black or gray jurisdiction is not just "bad fame", but some (not all) jurisdictions do not allow tax resident companies to deduct expenses when paid to companies formed in black labeled jurisdictions.

Capital Gains tax

Capital Gains Tax (CGT) is a tax on the profit realized from the sale of an asset that was purchased at a cost amount that was lower than the amount received on sale. The most common capital gains are realized from the sale of stocks, bonds, precious metals, real estate, and property. CGT is typically calculated on the difference between the purchase price (or acquisition cost) and the selling price (or disposal proceeds).

Typically, a Capital Gains Tax is not due until you sell or convert the asset.

Realized Capital Gains Tax

When you hold an asset, and it increases its value, you are not subject to Capital Gains Tax, until to sell that asset with a profit, meaning a Capital Gains Tax is not due, levied, or assessed until you sell the asset. To trigger a taxable event, there must be first a Realized "Capital Gain"

Capital Gains Tax Exemption

There is a common practice by jurisdictions, especially by tax havens, to not levy Capital Gains Tax on the sale of these type of assets. This can be by pure tax havens, or partial tax havens, where the jurisdiction exempts from Capital Gains Tax the profit from the sale or transfer of assets.

For example, Singapore has a 19% income tax rate on Singapore Sourced income, but it has a 0% income tax rate (tax exemption) on Capital Gains.

(Singapore is one of the tax havens with the most complex tax system, which allows them to be a tax haven while being white-listed and highly prestigious among foreign jurisdictions)

Not selling your assets in order to avoid incurring into a Realized Capital Gains event.

Unlike income tax which can be deemed as distributed by Controlled Foreign Companies Rules, Capital Gains is not taxed until the asset it sold at a gain, as the sale of the assets and the profits is considered a taxable event. If you don't sell or transfer these assets there is no taxable event.

Factors determining if an income is capital gain or regular business income

Percentage of overall income to determine if sale of asset is capital gain or regular income

Capital Gains tax generally means passive income, like earning rents from real estate property rental, dividends, etc., nonetheless, that income exceeds 50% of the company's overall income, it will not be considered and classified as capital gains, but as general business income, hence subject to income tax in case the jurisdiction taxes income tax.

How long you hold an asset might determine if the income would be treated as capital gains or regular income

Some jurisdictions, in addition to whether the profit from selling the assets represent 51%, there are other factors to determine if the sale of an asset is to be considered capital gains, even if such capital gains does not exceed the company's 50% overall income.

In general, some jurisdictions might not consider an income as capital gains, and classify it as regular business income, if you hold the asset for less than 1 year.

Trust to avoid capital gains tax or inheritance tax

When holding your assets under a Trust, the assets are managed under the benefit of the beneficiary, nonetheless, the beneficiary is not directly the owner of such assets, the owner is the Trust or a company or entity owned by the Trust. So when the settlor (the person who put the assets into the trust) dies, there is no change in the assets' ownership, hence the capital gains tax is not triggered as there is no change in the asset's ownership title by way of inheritance.

How and why do rich people or millionaires do not pay taxes? Buy Borrow Die Tax Strategy

Most rich people have their wealth from and invested in Real Estate, Stocks, Bonds, or any other capital assets. The income from such investments is taxed as a Capital Gain.

Capital Gains are the increase in value of an asset in comparison to your purchase price, and Capital gains are taxed at the moment it is a realized capital gain or, put simply, when the asset is sold.

As long as you hold the investment and don't sell it, the increase in value will be an unrealized capital gain, hence a taxable event will not be triggered.

So you bought Stocks, and now they are worth millions of dollars, or your real estate appreciated in value, and you don't want to sell them to now pay income tax, but you need cash to not be just rich on paper. What rich people do is they request a loan and they use their assets as a collateral or warranty. These loans are usually granted a low interest rest, and interest payments can also be deducted from income tax. A Win-Win situation.

There are, of course, other ways, strategies, and vehicles rich people use to not pay taxes or to reduce their tax bill, i.e. offshore company formation and trusts, personalized tax breaks, international tax planning, etc, as Capital Gain Tax is not the only that out there, but The Buy, Borrow, Die scheme is a simple and common tax strategy used by rich people to legally reduce their tax liability or prevent paying taxes.

The Contrast - Getting Paid in Salary

When an employee gets paid in salary and/or wages, the Employer withholds income and/or payroll tax from the employee at a 30% tax rate (the rate can vary from jurisdiction to jurisdiction, country to country, but we are using the 30% rate as an example only).

The taxable event is when you are paid your salary, so for a $100,000 salary, you will pay $30,000 in taxes.

How can anyone benefit from this?

Being rich does not mean you will not pay taxes if you are getting your income in the form of a salary, as you can be a rich CEO from a big company/bank earning million of dollars per year, but pay even a higher tax rate than those who earn less because salary and wages are usually taxed at a progressive tax.

It is just that the tax system seems to indirectly incentivize investments.

So even if you are not a millionaire, you could benefit from and implement this strategy as long as the tax you want to avoid is capital gain tax.

Important considerations:

This borrow die strategy might not work in some countries, especially in those that are considered high risk countries as their bank loan rates are usually higher than capital gains tax rate.

Digital assets like cryptocurrency are not a common asset used for this strategy as most banks will not take crypto as a debt warranty due to its high volatility.

Withholding tax

Withholding tax is a tax levied on payments made by a tax resident company to a non-resident company. For example, suppose you have a company in Country A, which imposes a 25% withholding tax. If Company B, a non-tax resident company before the eyes of Country A and incorporated in Country B receives royalty payments, rents, etc., from company A, these payments might be subject to ta withholding tax up to 30% (this varies per jurisdiction).

If a payment is not determined to be sourced from jurisdiction A, it will not be subject to withholding tax, even if the payor is from or the money is coming from that jurisdiction.

Company A is required to withhold XX% of the payment made to Company B because Company B is not a tax resident of Country A, and the type of income Company B is receiving from Company A is deemed to be sourced from Country A and it also is taxed (not exempt) in jurisdiction A. This means that Company A must deduct this tax from the payment and remit it to the tax authorities in Country A. The rationale behind this is that since Company B is not a tax resident in Country A, it will not file a yearly tax statement there. Therefore, the withholding tax ensures that the income earned by Company B from sources within Country A is taxed appropriately so it the tax does not escape.

Withholding tax nature is to avoid an income sourced from that country or jurisdiction to avoid taxation because non-resident countries are hard to pursue and make them declare their Country A sourced income, so to basically to avoid this hassle, and to also avoid artificial shift of profit between companies, Country A levies a withholding tax on Company B formed in Country B, and at a higher tax rate than tax resident companies formed in Country A.

One of the cons of being subject to withholding tax, besides paying taxes, is that withholding tax does not allow you to deduct costs or expenses related to generating that income, unlike companies considered tax resident in Country A

Ways to avoid withholding tax

Tax treaties.

We will explain this in one of the subchapters below

Forming a tax resident company in a Country A

Another way to avoid withholding tax is to form a tax resident company in Country A to avoid withholding tax, this way the income with not be taxed at the gross income value, but at the net income or less value.

This way you can use the company in Country A to pay for expenses for generating that income, paying costs, salaries, etc.,

A specific option to avoid withholding taxes from the European Union

The European Union has a specific tax system, where basically and put simple, there is no withholding tax when the payment is made to a company tax resident in another European Union Jurisdiction.

So if you were to receive income subject from a European Union Jurisdiction, by forming a company in Malta you can avoid this withholding tax, and only pay a 5% effective tax rate on your net income.

Exit Tax

There are jurisdictions where in order to stop being a tax resident, you need to either give up your center of vital interest, pay any capital gains and income tax accrued, or both.

Let's take Canada or the U.K. as an example. Unlike the U.S. you don't need to give up your tax passport to stop being a tax resident, but you need to stop having your center of vital interest in that jurisdiction, and to pay any capital gains tax accrued.

For example, let's say one year you brought some shares of Offshore Affairs INC at 10 USD per share., and now these shares are worth 1,000 USD each, and you haven't sold these shares yet. If you want to stop being a tax resident in Canada, or the U.K., you would have to pay an exit tax where the tax authority will deem that you sold the shares (which you didn't and still hold the shares), and they are deemed as being sold.

Not all jurisdictions have an exit tax procedure. This depends from jurisdictions to jurisdictions tax codes.

This does not only apply to shares, this also applies to any other type of property subject to capital gains tax, as cryptocurrency, your home or any other property, brands, etc.

That is why is it recommended to plan ahead and buy these shares under a tax shelter or strategy so when your assets increase in value they will not be subject to capital gains tax once you do an exit tax procedure. By planning ahead, you can legally avoid this capital gains tax when doing an exit tax procedure.

Besides paying taxes on any accrued capital gains, these jurisdictions might also require you to close any company, personal or business bank account, even gym memberships, located in that jurisdiction.

Tax Treaty

A tax treaty, also known as Double Taxation Avoidance Agreement or DTAA, is an agreement between two jurisdictions to avoid a Person/Resident (company or individual) being taxed twice, on the basis that such income should only be taxed in the jurisdiction where the Person is a tax resident in, except for that income generated at the source jurisdiction through a Permanent Establishment.

There are cases when a Person may be considered a tax resident in both countries, so in these cases the tax treaty sets out the rules to determine where the Person would ultimately be a tax resident in, for the treaty's purposes.

These DTAAs in general cover several taxes all at once, such as royalties, real estate income, capital gains, business income, employment income, etc., but these may vary, and the agreement may be just for a specific tax.

What is the benefit of a tax treaty? The benefit could be a full tax exemption, or a lower tax rate.

Most tax treaties are drafted, in general, using the OECD or EU model, but each one of them might have their own particularities.

Treaty shopping

What is treaty shopping?

Treaty shopping is picking a jurisdiction to form an offshore company in or to become a resident in merely for the purpose of benefiting from the jurisdiction's tax treaty network.

So for example, if you will have income from trading in China, you would have to check which jurisdictions China has a tax treaty with, and then send money to this offshore company with no withholding tax or with a lower rate. People mostly pick Hong Kong in this case because Hong Kong has a tax treaty with China, and also Hong Kong has it easier exchanging Renminbi.

If you were to do business in Ethiopia, you could form a company in Seychelles to receive the income tax free.

The above seems too simple, and it was in the past, now a lot of countries, tax havens, have implemented Economic Substance Requirements to certain activities and jurisdictions with low-tax rates.

Tax Treaty Resident Status

In order to benefit from a tax treaty, the company must be deemed to be a tax resident under the tax treaty.

Tax Treaties subscribed between jurisdictions grant a broad range of tax relieves for income tax (for companies and individuals), capital gain, gifts, royalties, etc. In order to benefit from the tax benefits of said tax treaties, you or your company must be a tax resident in one or both of the contracting parties and you can accomplish this by incorporating a company and obtaining a tax residency certificate.

Nonetheless, these tax treaties, most of the time but not always, have a rule which requires a person (company or individual) to be subject to tax not only on his/her income from that jurisdiction. This requirement is usually found on the Resident Definition clause, key factor to be able to benefit from the tax treaty. You may find a language similar to this: "This term (resident), however, does not include any person who is liable to tax in that State in respect only of income from sources in that State". Or "This term, however, does not include any person who is liable to tax in that State in respect only of income from sources in that State or capital situated therein."

As an example, if you form a company in Seychelles, and you want to benefit and access to the tax treaty network, you cannot form a company type in Seychelles that is supposed to pay 0% on its offshore income, because it will not be considered a Seychelles Tax Resident Company: on the other hand, you can form a Special License Company in Seychelles which is taxed at a 1.5% rate, and be able to be considered a tax resident.

As another example, Belize has the LLC which is not taxed so it cannot access tax treaty benefit, but it also has the IBC which is taxed at a 1.5% - 3% tax rate so this one can access the tax treaty network subscribed by Belize.

So, basically, if you form a company that is taxed at a 0% in BVI, it can be considered a tax resident in BVI under local laws, but it will not be considered a tax resident before the eyes of the Tax Treaties subscribed by BVI.

Minimum tax rate required

Sometimes tax treaties requires that the entity type not only be taxed on the worldwide income, but also that it be taxed at a minimum tax rate.

Some other jurisdictions exclude certain territories from some of their tax treaties subscribed. This is the case of Labuan, a Federal Territory of Malaysia, which has a 3% tax rate, but it is excluded from about 2 tax treaties subscribed by Malaysia due its low tax rate.

Maintenance price of low tax companies

The price for the yearly maintenance of these can be very high, in comparison to tax exempt companies.

By law, some of these companies, especially those taxed below 10%, are required to have one employee or more, rented office which in the country cannot be a virtual office or address, a minimum of yearly expenditures, etc., otherwise these companies would not be able to get the residency certificate.

So that is the logic of why in a tax haven you would rather pick a low tax entity, instead of a no tax or tax exempt company.

Just a few low tax entities and jurisdictions are the following:

Seychelles Special License Company: 1.5%

Labuan LTD: 3%

Mauritius GBL Company: 3%

Malta LTD: 5%

Barbados: 5.5%

Hungary KFT or OCC: 9%

Ireland LTD: 15.5

and so on...

Not all Low Tax Jurisdictions are subject to economic substance requirements to benefit from their tax residency and tax treaties.

There are jurisdictions where a X% income tax rate is applied to you, and residency is based on country of formation/incorporation, and not place of management, without the need to have Economic Substance in that country.

For example, companies formed in Malta are subject to an effective income tax rate of 5%, which allows you to trade under a European Union company, have access to its tax treaties, and without having to have economic substance in the country, like employees, office space or monthly expenditures in Malta.

Economic Substance Requirements

Economic Substance requirements must be taken into consideration, even if the company is taxed at a 0%, 10%, or even if you don't want to benefit from the tax treaty network.

Economic Substance Requirement are imposed on companies engaged in certain activities, basically to avoid forming a company in a jurisdiction just for the purpose of taking advantage of its tax system.

This also aims to avoid profit shifting.

It is important to note that Economic Substance Requirements do not apply to all businesses. For the Economic Substance Requirements, the company has meet two conditions:

1. Be a Tax Resident in that jurisdiction.

2. Be engaged in relevant activities.

If a Company is a tax resident in that jurisdiction, to know if the Economic Substance Requirements would apply is to know if the entity is engaged in Relevant activities. If the company is not a tax resident because, for example, has it place of management somewhere else, Economic Substance Requirements would not apply even if it is engaged in Relevant activities.

In general, Relevant Activities, most of the time, are:

- Banking business
- Insurance business
- Fund management business
- Finance and leasing business
- Headquarters business

- Shipping business

- Holding business (pure equity holding entities)

- Intellectual property (IP) business

- Distribution and service centre business (this includes providing services to related companies)

Of course, each jurisdiction will have its own list of Relevant Activities, and what is comprised in each one of them.

Profit Shifting

Profit shifting is moving your income from Company A located in Territory A to Company B located in Territory B. Territory B is a no tax or low tax jurisdiction, so at the end reporting the income in territory B will result in less taxes, while in territory A you will report as less net income as possible, and if possible you could even report your tax statement as having losses. Profit shifting is linked to base erosion

Base Erosion:

In general, you get taxed on your net income. Your net income is your gross income minus your costs and expenses. What results from this is your tax base to what the tax percentage will be applied on.

Base erosion is lowering your net income by increasing your

expenses, using profit shifting strategies, some of which are explained next.

Profit Shifting Strategies

Intellectual Property

Intellectual Property, like royalties or license payments, is one of the most commonly used method to shift profit from one jurisdiction to another since it is hard for tax authorities to put a price on your intellectual property (IP), and also because they are easier to justify. When I say put a price on your IP, for tax purposes it would hard for you to claim that you bought an iPhone for ten thousand dollars, the tax authority will value such expense (buying the cellphone) at a fair market value; on the other hand, it is harder for them to put a fair market value on your intellectual property (trading mark, logo, patent, copyright, etc.).

As a general rule, the Company incorporated in a low tax jurisdiction owns the Intellectual Property and grants a Use License to the trading company in the high tax jurisdiction. The Company in the high tax jurisdiction will send its profits to the Offshore company as an expense and deduct it from its gross income.

If you obtain 1,000,000 USD in net profits in Country A, you will be taxed at a rate of 30% for income tax (because income tax generally is a progressive tax) on that 1M. To reduce this tax bill, you send this profit to the Offshore Company where it will not pay taxes or pay less, but Country A may require you to withhold from that Offshore Company an amount on that Royalty payment, which is generally around 15%, sometimes even more. That is when the tax treaty comes in to avoid this withholding tax.

Services

Also, one of the most used, but probably one of the easiest way to shift profit to an offshore jurisdiction, especially because most of the time Professional Services paid to non-residents are withholding tax free.

If you do this, you also have to keep an eye on economic substance requirements on the offshore jurisdiction, as this can be considered a relevant activity as it is a service provided by the Offshore Company to a related party, hence acting as a Service Center.

Some people use some means like hiring the services of nominee shareholders of the offshore company so they are not seen as related entities and hence not fall under the Relevant Activity concept. This can be tax evasion.

For profit shifting, you have to make sure the country where the income is going is not blacklisted in the country where you want to deduct these payments, otherwise.

Loans

Loans are widely used to reduce the tax base. The strategy consists of you grating a loan between a related party, at a high-interest rate, being then that interest payment registered as an expense for the loan grantee.

Loans are used by multinationals (a company owning a company in another jurisdiction) to transfer profits by way of interest payments because such interest in registered as an expense in the objective base erosion company.

Hybrid loans are loans that take advantage of two jurisdictions tax code mismatch which allows the whole transaction to not be taxed for either party.

Several jurisdictions have implanted rules to regulate hybrid loans in order to reduce tax avoidance, for example setting up a maximum interest rate, related parties rules, loan maturity period, etc.

The above is just said in an easy way. In practice, some countries are implementing an OECD Plan to avoid Base Erosion, which makes it harder for companies to engage in base erosion practice. It is possible to erode the tax base, but a high knowledge of the international tax law, and the countries involved tax code, is needed.

CFC Rules

Have you ever wondered if you can open an offshore company, operate through this entity, and keep the money in this entity without paying taxes where you reside as you won't pay yourself distribution/dividends (unrealized taxable event)? The answer to this can be found, most of the time, in the Controlled Foreign Company rules.

Controlled Foreign Company (CFC) Rules are legislations that require tax residents to report certain income of Companies incorporated in a jurisdiction different than the CFC Ruled jurisdiction.

The purpose of CFC rules is to combat artificial deferral of tax by using offshore low taxed entities through profit shifting strategies.

These rules vary depending of your country of tax residency, but in general they require you to report any interest or income from a company from which you hold certain percentage of ownership. The percentage may go from 10% ownership to 50%+.

A way to avoid CFC Rules, in case your jurisdiction of Tax Residency has CFC Rules, is to divert and dilute ownership between individuals so you don't meet the threshold to be report this company under CFC Rules.

Transfer Pricing

Transfer pricing is a pivotal aspect of international tax planning for multinational corporations (MNCs), governing how transactions among related entities across different jurisdictions are priced. At its core lies the arm's length principle, requiring transactions between related parties to be priced as if they were conducted between independent, unrelated entities. This principle aims to prevent artificial profit shifting and ensure fair allocation of profits and taxes globally.

Key methods used to determine transfer prices include the Comparable Uncontrolled Price (CUP), Cost Plus Method (CPM), Resale Price Method (RPM), and Profit Split Method (PSM). These methods involve comparing prices with similar transactions among unrelated parties or applying markups and profit splits that reflect each entity's contributions and economic realities.

Documentation is crucial in transfer pricing. MNCs must maintain detailed records and economic analyses supporting their transfer pricing policies. This documentation not only justifies the selection of pricing methods but also demonstrates compliance with local regulations and international standards, such as those set by the OECD.

In terms of international tax planning, transfer pricing offers strategic advantages. It allows MNCs to optimize their tax liabilities by allocating profits to jurisdictions with favorable tax rates while ensuring adherence to regulatory requirements in each country. Compliance efforts include navigating complex regulations, adhering to OECD guidelines, and managing bilateral tax treaties to minimize tax risks and promote transparency.

Advance Pricing Agreements (APAs) provide additional certainty to MNCs by establishing agreed-upon transfer pricing methods and prices with tax authorities in advance. This reduces the likelihood of tax audits and adjustments, providing stability and predictability in tax planning.

What are related entities under the transfer pricing rules?

Related entities refer to entities that have a close relationship, typically due to ownership or control by the same parent company or shareholders. In the context of transfer pricing, related entities often include subsidiaries, branches, joint ventures, or other entities within a corporate group structure. These entities engage in transactions with each other, such as the sale of goods, provision of services, or licensing of intellectual property.

The transfer pricing rules of each jurisdiction will provide how much ownership percentage an individual or company, or mix of them, must have for a company to be considered a related entity.

The arm's length principle in transfer pricing aims to ensure that transactions between related entities are conducted on terms and conditions that would be agreed upon by unrelated parties in a similar situation. This principle prevents related entities from artificially shifting profits between jurisdictions to minimize tax liabilities. By pricing transactions at arm's length, MNCs strive to achieve a fair allocation of profits and taxes globally, reflecting economic realities rather than tax optimization strategies.

Arm's length principle

The Arm's Length Principle refers to the transactions where there is a manipulation or influence of contracts or transactions price where Company A and Company B, which are managed by related parties, set a price for these transactions at a favorable price, in order to manipulate the taxable rate at their convenience.

Under the transfer pricing rules. the transactions, under the arm's lengths principle, meaning the transactions or contracts influenced by a common owner, manager, controller, etc., of two or more companies, shall be priced at a price which is normal under independent companies where the owner, manager, controller., etc., is a different person or company.

At its core, this principle mandates that transactions between related parties must mirror those between independent, unrelated entities under similar circumstances. This approach ensures that economic realities, rather than internal considerations, dictate pricing decisions.

Central to applying the arm's length principle is the concept of fair market value. It requires transactions to be priced at levels that would prevail in a competitive market where parties are not related. This principle emphasizes comparability, where prices charged for goods, services, or intellectual property transferred between related entities are benchmarked against prices in comparable transactions involving unrelated parties. Methods like the Comparable Uncontrolled Price (CUP), Cost Plus Method (CPM), Resale Price Method (RPM), and Profit Split Method (PSM) are employed to achieve this comparability and determine appropriate transfer prices.

Tax Information Exchange Agreements

Tax Information Exchange Agreements (TIAEs) are bilateral or multilateral treaties subscribed by two or more jurisdictions where the requester Party can request the Requested Party to share the tax information they have on an investigated individual. These TIAEs cover specifically which taxes will be covered for information exchange purposes, requirements to request such information, cases where the Requested Party can deny cooperating, allowing a representative of the Requester Party to enter the Territory of the Requested Party and be able to interview individuals and inspect tax other relevant records, among other provisions.

Most TIAEs are based on the OECD Model Agreement on Exchange of Information on Tax Matters.

TIAEs can also be found within Double Taxation Avoidance Agreements.

To confirm if a jurisdiction has signed a TIAE with a specific jurisdiction, you would have to check on a case by case basis.

Now that you know the basics of international tax planning, let's review one of most popular international tax strategies

Double Irish Dutch Sandwich Tax Avoidance Explained

The Double Irish with Dutch Sandwich is one of the most popular tax avoidance schemes as it is used by the biggest tech companies such as Apple, Facebook, Google, Microsoft, etc., taking profit from legal mismatches and loopholes. The name of the scheme comes from setting up two Irish subsidiaries and one Dutch company in the middle of the tax structure.

How does the scheme work? first, it is necessary to point out that the U.S tax system does not tax the U.S, Companies who do not repatriate dividends from foreign subsidiaries (Tax Cuts and Jobs Act), hence a US company sets up two Irish companies, Subsidiary 1 and Subsidiary 2.

Why are the foreign subsidiaries set up in Ireland? Because pursuant to the Irish tax system a company can be tax resident by place of management, not country of incorporation if the company is controlled by another company residing in a country that has a double tax treaty with Ireland.

Subsidiary 1 will have its place of management in a pure tax haven (0% on income tax) to avoid being an Irish tax resident, and Subsidiary 2 will be a tax resident in Ireland and will carry trade and bring profit (income) from sales.

Now that we have the 2 Irish companies set up, the U.S. company grants a license to Subsidiary 1 to exploit certain intellectual property, and Subsidiary 1 will license said intellectual property to Subsidiary 2 who will generate real profit from real sales.

If Subsidiary 2 sends the resulting dividends directly to Subsidiary 1, as you might have guessed, the income could be liable for Irish withholding tax, and there is where and why the Dutch subsidiary comes in.

To avoid the Irish withholding tax on dividends, a Dutch Subsidiary is set up and Subsidiary 2 will send the dividends from sales directly to the Dutch Subsidiary, and the Dutch Subsidiary will send the dividends tax-free to Subsidiary 1. **But why is it tax-free?** Because under EC Directive 2003/49 interests and royalty payments made by a company in a member state to a company in **another** member state are tax-free.

Disclaimer: the tax concepts in this chapter are explained as generic and simple as possible, being the purpose of this Chapter for you to have a superficial knowledge of some tax terms involved in the offshore affairs. You must understand that each tax concept can be deeply studied in a thousand pages book, but at the end of the day the final word will be the definition contained in each jurisdiction tax code, tax treaties, etc.

Final Thoughts

Thank you for reading this book! I hope that now you are able to understand how offshore companies and tax havens work in general when it comes to international taxation and are able to investigate further by yourself your tax status, applicable rules and regulations. And also, if you are going to hire the services of a international tax lawyer, you will be able to ask more substantial questions, profiting at the maximum the hourly rate you pay for international tax counseling.

Company Important Links

Offshore Affairs Website

www.offshoreaffairs.com

Twitter

https://x.com/OffshoreAffairs

YouTube

www.youtube.com/@OffshoreAffairs

Offshore Affairs LinkedIn

https://www.linkedin.com/company/offshoreaffairs

Jean Franco Fernandez Clark's Contact

LinkedIn

https://www.linkedin.com/in/jeanffc94/

X/ Twitter

https://x.com/jffc94

www.ingramcontent.com/pod-product-compliance
Lightning Source LLC
Chambersburg PA
CBHW030454220526
45464CB00006B/2529